D0736176

**Second Edition**

THE MANAGER'S POCKET GUIDE TO

# Recruiting the Workforce of the Future

*Bruce Tulgan*

## HRD PRESS
**Amherst, Massachusetts**

Published by:   HRD Press, Inc.
                22 Amherst Road
                Amherst, MA 01002
                800-822-2801 (U.S. and Canada)
                413-253-3488
                413-253-3490 (fax)
                http://www.hrdpress.com

ISBN: 0-87425-600-3

Cover design by Eileen Klockars
Editorial and production services by Mary George

## ❧ Dedication

*This book is dedicated to*
***Debby Applegate***, *the star*
*performer in my life.*

# Contents

# Acknowledgments

**As always,** thanks first and foremost to the many thousands of incredible people who have shared with me over the years the lessons of their experiences in the workplace.

I also want to thank all of the business leaders and managers who have expressed so much confidence in our work at RainmakerThinking and who have given us the opportunity to learn from the real management issues they deal with and solve on a daily basis.

To the tens of thousands who have attended my seminars, I once again say thanks for listening, for laughing, for sharing the wisdom of your experience, for pushing me with the really tough questions, for all of your kindness, and for continually teaching me.

Many thanks as well to Bob Carkhuff and HRD Press. We couldn't ask for better partners in the training business. And Mary George is a most awesome editor and designer: thank you.

To my colleagues at RainmakerThinking, especially Cynthia Conrad, Jeff Coombs, Mark Kurber,

Carolyn Martin, and Heather Neely, thank you for your hard work and commitment and for your valuable contributions to this enterprise every single day. Special thanks to Kelly Poggio and Jeff Hockenbrock, who put so much hard work into the appendix.

To my family and friends, I owe you my deep thanks for being you and for allowing me to be who I am. And as always, I reserve my greatest thanks for my wife, Debby Applegate, who is my best friend, my partner in all things, and the owner of my heart.

# Introduction

EVERY ORGANIZATION IN EVERY INDUSTRY is now spending more time, more energy, and more money than ever before recruiting the talent they need to compete in today's high-speed, high-tech, knowledge-driven, globally defined, and rapidly changing business market. There is tremendous pressure to recruit high-quality people because in a lean, post-downsizing organization in the midst of a tight labor market, managers need to get more work done, and better work done, with fewer people. But the supply of skilled workers is simply not growing fast enough, at any level, to meet the growing needs of organizations. That's why the competition for high-quality workers is so intense at every level of the labor market.

Skilled employees are in such great demand, and employers are so concerned about retaining them and getting a decent return on recruiting and training investments, that employees have more negotiating power in the workplace than ever before. Many employers are putting more resources and creativity into the competition for talent than they are putting into the competition for customers.

Sweetened deals, including higher-than-usual starting salaries, accelerated raises and promotions, and even retention bonuses, are becoming more and more common. Suddenly, it seems that no perk is off the table.

Managers and business leaders everywhere are trying to figure out how to solve this staffing crisis. *Recruiting the Workforce of the Future* and its related training program are designed to lend a helping hand with developing and implementing solutions. Their fundamental message is that employers should no longer be recruiting for the long term, but rather, recruiting to get the job done *today, tomorrow, and next week;* beyond that, staffing needs are unpredictable.

Throughout most of the industrial era and until recently, the dominant staffing model for most employers was based on long-term, full-time, on-site employment relationships. But in today's quickly changing marketplace, where employers can never predict what is just around the corner, the old-fashioned, stable, till-retirement-do-us-part employer-employee relationship simply doesn't fit. The key to continued success for companies now is the ability to adapt rapidly to new circumstances. Staffing may have to expand quickly in one skill area, or contract quickly in another—or do both at the same time. Strategies for staffing must therefore be geared to this reality.

The best practices outlined in this pocket guide are presented as keys and processes, and supplemented with worksheets and checklists. They are intended to give you an advantage when it comes to quickly and effectively bringing in the talent you need when you need it. Chapters 1 through 4 each focus on a series of best practices in a particular area:

➤ **Profiling:** How to develop quick skill-and-performance-based profiles of the people you are trying to hire, including a checklist of skills to look for in the workforce of the future.

➤ **The Recruiting Message:** How to create a message that is compelling to workers in today's economy, including the job factors most sought after by workers of the future.

➤ **The Recruiting Campaign:** How to execute a full-scale campaign to compete with the most zealous employers, including a whole set of guidelines for creating a recruiting campaign plan.

➤ **Selection:** How to select people based on nothing but skill and performance criteria, including tips for interviewing, getting candidates to submit proposals, and providing realistic job previews.

Chapter 5 reviews the most important points of the best practices.

Over time, I have shared this approach to recruiting with thousands of business leaders all over the world, in speeches and in my work with many of our clients. Because so many clients have asked for more resources to teach managers the approach, I have developed a full-scale management training program based on this pocket guide, to be published as the latest in our ongoing series with HRD Press.

This second edition of *Recruiting the Workforce of the Future* offers you many of the new insights I gained from creating the training program. They are presented through these important features:

➤ *Clear and simple explanations*

➤ *Examples from real-life workplace case studies*

➤ *Concrete action steps*

➤ *Room for productive brainstorming*

➤ *Helpful tools for planning to implement the action steps*

Also, an extensive list of Web-based resources has been included in the appendix, to help you explore the wide array of recruiting services available through the Internet.

It is my hope that by using this second edition as your guide, you will gain the distinct advantage of getting the talent needed to get the work done in your organization.

# Profiling the Employee of the Future

**MANY EMPLOYERS ARE STILL USING** employee profiles they developed five, ten, or fifteen years ago—sometimes even longer. While most of these profiles are based on valid research into personality traits, most are also based on an obsolete assumption: that long-term employment is one of the goals of hiring.

Often less formal profiles are used as well. These reside in the minds of business leaders and managers, and may best be described as *employer self-profiles.* In essence, leaders and managers tend to look for employees who think and behave as they once did (or as they recall they once did). Thus many employers, whether consciously or not, look for employees who are willing to "pay their dues and climb the ladder." But times and requirements have changed. Employers today need employees who are ready to get the work done, whenever they can, wherever they can, however they can, whatever the work may be on any given day.

In the new economy, the people who are in greatest demand—flexible, adaptable, information-savvy, technoliterate, rapid-learning, innovative and independent entrepreneurs—are also the least likely to be attached to the old-fashioned, long-term career path. So it is a mistake to look for employees who want to follow the old protocol: going to work every day in the same building during the same hours to do the same tasks in the same position with the same responsibility in the same chain of command.

Strict adherence to the job description, obedience to authority, and loyalty to the organization are no longer the most valuable traits in employees. In fact, these traits may well undermine the critical thinking, personal initiative, and ad hoc team building that is so essential for success in today's rapidly changing workplace.

## 0━ THE KEY

In the workplace of the future, it is critical to discard obsolete recruiting and hiring criteria. The only thing that matters is this: Can the person get the work done—accomplish the results you need—quickly and at a high level of quality? Profiling should be based *only* on skill and performance criteria.

## ▶▶ THE PROCESS

- Reassess traditional credential requirements for each task and responsibility.

  (You may find that many of the necessary tasks
  and responsibilities do not, in fact, require
  any particular credentials.)

- Develop profiles on the basis of skill and
  performance criteria.

- Brainstorm using the checklist of critical
  skills for workers of the future, provided
  later in this chapter.

## ▶▶ Reassess Traditional Credential Requirements

1. What tasks must be achieved, and what
   responsibilities must be fulfilled?

2. What are the required credentials?

3. Why are those credentials required? Are you
   sure they are required?

*Use the worksheet to record your answers.*

## WORKSHEET

### Reassess Traditional Credential Requirements

| THE WORK: Tasks & Responsibilities | Required Credentials | Why? Are you sure? |
|---|---|---|
|  |  |  |
|  |  |  |
|  |  |  |
|  |  |  |

(Continued)

**WORKSHEET** (Concluded)

## Reassess Traditional Credential Requirements

| THE WORK:<br>Tasks &<br>Responsibilities | Required<br>Credentials | Why?<br>Are you sure? |
|---|---|---|
|  |  |  |
|  |  |  |
|  |  |  |

 Take note of which tasks and responsibilities require credentials and which do not. For a few minutes, question your assumptions about the position you need to fill. If, for example, only a small portion of the work requires credentials, it may be wise to segregate those tasks and responsibilities and assign them to a current staff person who has those credentials, thereby freeing your hiring process from the requirement.

## ➡ Profile the Position Based on Skill and Performance Criteria

1. What tasks and responsibilities define the work?

2. What skills and abilities are required?

*Use the following worksheet to record your profile.*

**Please note!**

The critical skills checklist in the next section of this chapter may be a useful reference point for completing the worksheet.

**WORKSHEET**

## Profile Based on Skill & Performance Criteria

| THE WORK: Tasks & Responsibilities | Skills & Abilities |
|---|---|
|  |  |

(Continued)

**WORKSHEET** (Concluded)

## Profile Based on Skill & Performance Criteria

| THE WORK:<br>Tasks & Responsibilities | Skills & Abilities |
|---|---|
| | |

## ➤➤ Brainstorm the Required Skills

The list below will help you brainstorm the skills
needed for the position you are profiling. Consider
each skill and determine its importance to the job.
When you identify an important skill, elaborate:
How is the skill essential to the position in question?

✓ **CHECKLIST**

*Critical Skills to Look for in
the Workforce of the Future\**

## Learning Skills

1. **Voracious Learning.** The desire and ability to
   devour and process information rapidly, to
   get up to speed on new skills and knowledge,
   and to stay ahead of the rapidly accelerating
   obsolescence curve.

   ❑ *Elaborate:*

2. **Multi-Tasking.** The ability to juggle many
   different images, sounds, and texts coming
   from different sides all at once.

   ❑ *Elaborate:*

\*These are the most important skills in workers today, based on
the ongoing research conducted by RainmakerThinking, Inc.

3. **Strategic Learning.** The ability to sort through the vast tidal wave of information in today's world and make acute decisions about what one is going to throw out and what one is going to learn.

   ❏ *Elaborate:*

4. **Information Management.** The ability to frame research inquiries, effectively access information resources, gather worthwhile data, store data in an organized manner for easy recall, and use data effectively.

   ❏ *Elaborate:*

5. **Critical Thinking.** The ability to differentiate between reliable and unreliable information, carefully weigh the strengths of conflicting views, and make reasoned judgments. The habit of taking the time to consider various possibilities and not become too attached to one point of view. Balancing an openness to the views of others with independent judgment.

   ❏ *Elaborate:*

6. **Foreign Language Mastery.**

   ❏ *Elaborate:*


7. **Technoliteracy.** The desire and ability to learn and operate new technologies.

   ❏ *Elaborate:*


8. **Protégé Behavior.** Being the diligent protégé of a worthy mentor. Studying the example of an accomplished, experienced, and wise person whom one admires.

   ❏ *Elaborate:*


*Additional Learning Skills*

Are there additional learning skills you want to add to this checklist? If so, record them below.

## Relationship Skills

9. **Supply Focus in Relationships.** Approaching relationships in terms of what one has to offer others, instead of what one needs or wants from others.

   ❑ *Elaborate:*

10. **Seeking Out Decision-Makers.** Clarifying the decisions that must be made in order to reach specific goals, and then identifying the individuals who have the authority to make those decisions (or the influence to affect those decisions).

    ❑ *Elaborate:*

11. **Total Customer-Service Mindset.** Treating everyone as a customer — co-workers, employees, managers, suppliers, service people, and actual customers. Anticipating the needs of others and seeking to address them with cheerful promptness.

    ❑ *Elaborate:*

12. **Trustworthiness.** Spelling out expectations and assuming an absolute duty to fulfill those expectations. Being honest, realistic, responsible, on time, and accountable.

   ❑ *Elaborate:*

13. **Empathy.** The ability to imagine oneself in another person's position and tune in to the thoughts and feelings that person might have.

   ❑ *Elaborate:*

14. **Motivating Others.** The ability to visualize positive results and then enthusiastically share that positive vision in a way that inspires others.

   ❑ *Elaborate:*

15. **Facilitating the Effectiveness of Others.** The ability to train and coach others, set goals and deadlines, provide effective feedback, and reward good performance.

   ❑ *Elaborate:*

16. **Celebrating the Success of Others.** Giving people credit for their achievements, no matter how small those achievements, and trying to catch people doing things right.

    ❑ *Elaborate:*

17. **Being a Mentor.** Helping another person learn and grow and, in the process, practicing one's own leadership skills—priority setting, communication, and motivation.

    ❑ *Elaborate:*

18. **Communication.** Most important, the ability to listen or read carefully and understand what others are thinking and feeling and expressing. Also the ability to speak or write clearly and make oneself understood.

    ❑ *Elaborate:*

19. **Being a Great Team Player.** The practice of sacrificing one's own autonomy and contributing one's best ideas and hardest work to pursue a shared purpose along with others; giving up some individual recognition in

order to win recognition for the group and
its shared purpose.

❏ *Elaborate:*

20. **Negotiation and Conflict Resolution.** The
ability to handle conflicts; to clarify one's
own bottom line, identify the true bottom
line of another, expose the common ground,
and move oneself and another to that common ground.

❏ *Elaborate:*

*ADDITIONAL RELATIONSHIP SKILLS*

Are there additional relationship skills you want
to add to this checklist? If so, record them below.

❏ _____

❏ _____

❏ _____

❏ _____

❏ _____

❏ _____

## Value-Adding Skills

21. **Results Focus in Work.** The ability and inclination to organize one's work around clear tangible goals and concrete deadlines.

    ❏ *Elaborate:*

22. **Problem Identification.** Identifying problems that have not yet been identified.

    ❏ *Elaborate:*

23. **Problem Solving.** Solving problems that have not yet been solved.

    ❏ *Elaborate:*

24. **Improving Existing Services and Products.** Making them faster, more effective, more efficient, of higher quality, or less expensive.

    ❏ *Elaborate:*

25. **Inventing New Services and Products.**

    ❏ *Elaborate:*

26. **Being a Workhorse.** Putting in lots of time and energy in order to steadily accomplish many tasks that may be routine, menial, or even tedious.

❏ *Elaborate:*

27. **Seizing Opportunities to Add Value.** This includes being able to identify needs and match one's skills to those needs. The ability to define the value one is capable of adding and then create an effective sales message to persuade decision-makers to authorize and/or pay for the project.

❏ *Elaborate:*

28. **Deal Closing.** The ability to effectively engage in the process of deal closing: to clarify the parameters of a proposed transaction, identify the desired result of each party, move both parties to the common ground and eliminate mutually exclusive elements, and secure a binding agreement of both parties to execute the transaction.

❏ *Elaborate:*

29. **Strategic Planning.** The ability to identify many possible contingencies and to create, for each one, a plan to achieve clear goals by concrete deadlines; also the ability to utilize resources, overcome obstacles, and map out intermediate goals, deadlines, and necessary actions.

   ❑ *Elaborate:*

30. **Going the Extra Mile.** Consistently achieving more than one promises to achieve.

   ❑ *Elaborate:*

31. **Quality.** Holding oneself to a high standard. Thinking before speaking; outlining before writing (and always doing second drafts); planning before acting; double- and triple-checking before finalizing anything.

   ❑ *Elaborate:*

32. **Integrity.** A commitment to act on one's best knowledge and intentions, to be honest with oneself and with others, and to remain faithful to basic ethical principles.

    ❏ *Elaborate:*

33. **Speed.** The ability to beat established deadlines without compromising quality.

    ❏ *Elaborate:*

34. **Gauging Change.** The practice of monitoring feedback from every source to keep track of what is changing and what is staying the same, what is still working and what is no longer working.

    ❏ *Elaborate:*

35. **Flexibility.** The willingness and ability to continually make adjustments in one's goals, plans, and practices every step of the way as indicated by changing circumstances.

    ❏ *Elaborate:*

36. **Adaptability**. The ability and willingness to learn new skills, perform new tasks, do old tasks in new ways, and work with new machines, new managers, new co-workers, new customers, new rules, no rules; to do whatever is needed, whenever it's needed; to go, on any given day, from one boss to another, from one team to another, from one organization to another, from one set of tasks to another.

❑ *Elaborate:*

*ADDITIONAL VALUE-ADDING SKILLS*

Are there additional value-adding skills you want to add to this checklist? If so, record them below.

❑ _____

❑ _____

❑ _____

❑ _____

❑ _____

❑ _____

# 2

# Developing a Compelling Recruiting Message

**RECRUITING IS JUST LIKE SALES.** The first step is to develop a "sales" message compelling enough to attract a large applicant pool. The problem is, many employers offer nothing more than the same long-term career opportunities they've been offering for decades, and so their message falls flat. Today, the rewards of the old-fashioned career path — advancement in the organization's hierarchy, six-month reviews, annual raises, and other standard benefits — are simply not enough to attract the best talent. Such rewards are merely the threshold test: the cost of getting potential employees to consider you as a potential employer.

Brand yourself as employer. Take the example of the United States Marine Corps, which is the only branch of service in the United States military that has consistently met its recruiting and retention goals. How do they do that? The Marine Corps is a killer brand: Join the Marine Corps and they will transform you from head to toe. That happens to be the case with every branch of the service. But only the Marines have managed to convey that message effectively in the marketplace for talent.

For many employers, the biggest problem with "brand" in the marketplace for talent is that they are offering the same long-term career opportunities they have been offering for decades, and only that.

If all you have to sell are rewards that don't vest until several years into the future, then even the most carefully developed sales message will fail to compel. People in today's workforce want to know what you have to offer them today, tomorrow, next week, and next month in return for their added value.

## The Eight Essential Factors

There are eight factors that workers of the future look for in offers of employment:

1. *Performance-Based Compensation*
2. *Flexible Schedules*
3. *Flexible Location*
4. *Marketable Skills*
5. *Access to Decision-Makers*

6. *Personal Credit for Results Achieved*

7. *A Clear Area of Responsibility*

8. *The Chance for Creative Expression*

Let's take a closer look at each of these essential factors.

1. **Performance-Based Compensation.** Those in greatest demand today want to know that their compensation is not limited by any factor other than their own performance. People want to be assured that if they work harder and better they will be rewarded in direct proportion to the value they add. This is much more important to them than the amount of financial compensation they receive, though, of course, that amount must be in line with what is generally available in the marketplace.

2. **Flexible Schedules.** People want to know that as long as they are meeting goals and deadlines, they will have some control over their own schedules. The more control, the better.

3. **Flexible Location.** People want to know that as long as they are meeting goals and deadlines, they will have some control over where they work. If working in a particular space in a particular building will be required to any extent,

then it is important to assure people that they will have some power to define their own space (for instance, to arrange furniture, computers, art work, lighting, and so forth, to their liking).

4. **Marketable Skills.** People are looking for formal and informal training opportunities; they also want to be assured they will be building skills and knowledge continuously, at a rate that outpaces obsolescence.

5. **Access to Decision-Makers.** Those in today's workforce don't want to wait until they climb the ladder to build relationships with important leaders, managers, clients, customers, vendors, or co-workers. They want access right away.

6. **Personal Credit for Results Achieved.** Nobody wants to work hard to make somebody else look good. People want to put their own names on the tangible results they produce.

7. **A Clear Area of Responsibility.** People want to know that they will have 100 percent control of something, *anything,* so they can use that area of responsibility as their personal proving ground.

8. **The Chance for Creative Expression.** People want a clear picture of all the guidelines and

parameters that will constrain their creativity so they can imagine the terrain in which they will have freedom to do things their own way.

**O⇥ THE KEY**

Create a compelling recruiting message by answering the number one question of potential recruits:

### *What's the deal?*

*Or: Exactly what do you want me to do today, tomorrow, next week, and this month; and exactly what do you have to offer me in the form of financial and nonfinancial rewards today, tomorrow, next week, and this month?*

**▶ THE PROCESS**

- Evaluate your traditional rewards; then identify the ones that vest in the near term.

- Brainstorm the nontraditional incentives you have to offer.

  Using the eight factors that matter most to workers of the future, brainstorm incentives, particularly those you have to offer in the near term.

- Clarify exactly what you want from the person you are hiring.

- Develop a *What's the Deal?* recruiting message for each position that you are selling.

## ➡ Evaluate Your Traditional Rewards and Identify Those That Vest in the Near-Term

1. What traditional rewards are you able to offer?

2. Within what time period does each reward vest?

---

*Use the following worksheet to start building your recruiting message.*

---

**WORKSHEET**

## Evaluating Your Traditional Rewards

| TRADITIONAL REWARDS | Within What Time Period Does Each Reward Vest? | | | |
|---|---|---|---|---|
| Salary & Benefits | Right Away | 6 to 18 months | 18 to 36 months | 36 to 60 months |
| | | | | |
| | | | | |
| | | | | |
| | | | | |
| | | | | |
| | | | | |
| | | | | |

(Continued)

## WORKSHEET (Concluded)

### Evaluating Your Traditional Rewards

| TRADITIONAL REWARDS<br><br>Salary & Benefits | Within What Time Period Does Each Reward Vest? | | | |
|---|---|---|---|---|
| | Right Away | 6 to 18 months | 18 to 36 months | 36 to 60 months |
| | | | | |
| | | | | |
| | | | | |
| | | | | |
| | | | | |

 In building your recruiting message, be sure to emphasize the rewards that vest sooner, rather than later. The sooner a reward vests, the more compelling it will be as part of your recruiting message; the later a reward vests, the less compelling it will be. Rewards that vest longer than 60 months from the hiring date should not be emphasized at all.

## ➠ Brainstorm the Nontraditional Incentives You Have to Offer

Use the categories given below to brainstorm a list of incentives you can make available to new employees and, therefore, include in your recruiting message. Note whether the incentives you identify will be available to new employees immediately or not.

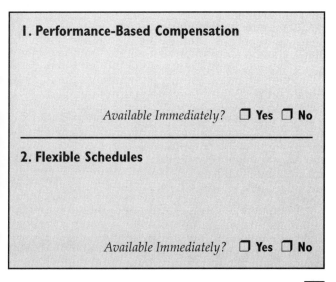

**1. Performance-Based Compensation**

*Available Immediately?*   ☐ **Yes** ☐ **No**

**2. Flexible Schedules**

*Available Immediately?*   ☐ **Yes** ☐ **No**

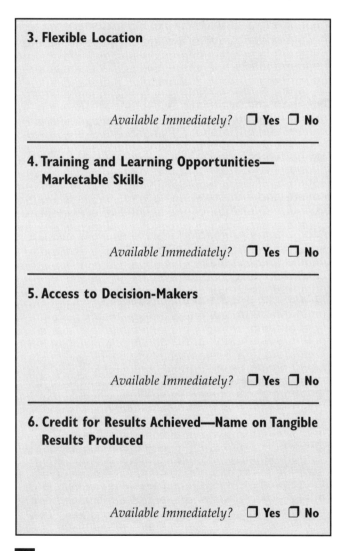

**3. Flexible Location**

*Available Immediately?*  ☐ **Yes** ☐ **No**

**4. Training and Learning Opportunities—Marketable Skills**

*Available Immediately?*  ☐ **Yes** ☐ **No**

**5. Access to Decision-Makers**

*Available Immediately?*  ☐ **Yes** ☐ **No**

**6. Credit for Results Achieved—Name on Tangible Results Produced**

*Available Immediately?*  ☐ **Yes** ☐ **No**

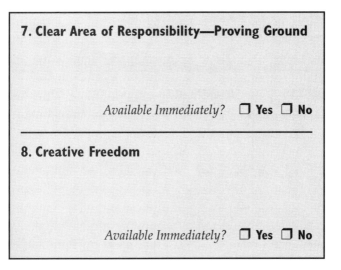

**7. Clear Area of Responsibility—Proving Ground**

*Available Immediately?* ☐ **Yes** ☐ **No**

**8. Creative Freedom**

*Available Immediately?* ☐ **Yes** ☐ **No**

 Review the incentives you have brain-stormed, especially those that vest right away. Choose the most unique, compelling incentives to include in your recruiting message.

## ➥ Clarify Exactly What You Want from the Person You Are Hiring

What tasks, responsibilities, projects, and other things do you expect from this person?

*Use the following worksheet to record your answers.*

**WORKSHEET**

## Clarifying What You Want from Recruits

| TASKS | RESPONSIBILITIES | PROJECTS | OTHER |
|-------|------------------|----------|-------|
|       |                  |          |       |

**➡ Develop Your Recruiting Message:**
*"What's the Deal?"*

1. What will you need from the start, or soon
   thereafter?

2. What will you offer from the start, or soon
   thereafter?

Create your "What's the Deal?" message based on
the message-building worksheets you've completed
thus far. Direct the message to potential recruits.

*This is what we'll need from you on day
one, or soon thereafter.*

*This is what we have to offer you on day one, or soon thereafter.*

_____

_____

_____

_____

_____

_____

_____

➤ **Stretch Goal:**

*How does that message help you shape your "brand" as an employer?*

---

*Be sure to create a compelling recruiting message for each position you are selling.*

# Planning Your Recruiting Campaign

**To be effective in today's** competitive labor market, your recruiting campaign must be an aggressive, year-round effort. That means all company materials, even sales materials, should be developed with recruiting goals in mind. It is important to communicate in everything the organization does that the organization is not just a great provider of goods and services, but also a great place to work. This is especially true when it comes to the organization's website, as potential applicants will visit your site at least as often as potential customers. And remember that recruiting messages reinforce sales goals: Clients and customers want to do business with an organization that is an employer of choice because happy employees produce better quality work and deliver better service.

It's also important to involve employees throughout the organization in the recruiting campaign, not just the recruiting team. That gives the mission a sense of urgency and high energy level that any campaign needs to be successful. Many employers even reward their employees with a cash bounty for bringing in new recruits (most require the new recruit to stick around for a period of time before the bounty is paid). While people appreciate the cash rewards, the real value of these efforts is the widespread involvement they generate.

In the midst of today's fierce talent wars, the most zealous and well-resourced employers are setting up full-time campaign headquarters with full-time staffs and the resources to wage a continuous recruiting effort. Of course, few employers have the resources to devote to a full-scale campaign. In either case, full-scale or not, the basic elements of a campaign are the same and will lead to a more robust applicant pool for your organization.

## ⊶ THE KEY

The goal of any recruiting campaign is quite simple:

> *Deliver the most compelling message to*
> *large concentrations of potential employees*
> *in order to draw them into your applicant pool.*

### ▶→ THE PROCESS

- Identify your target market(s). Decide who will be the audience for your message: Can you describe the target market(s) in specific terms?

- Identify the best means of direct and indirect communication with your target market(s).

- Determine your resources: What resources will be available to run the campaign?

- Plan and execute the campaign.

- Manage the campaign.

### ▶→ Identify Your Target Market(s)

1. Who will be the audience for your message?

2. Can you describe the target market(s) in specific terms?

---

*The following worksheet will help you develop your answers to these questions.*

---

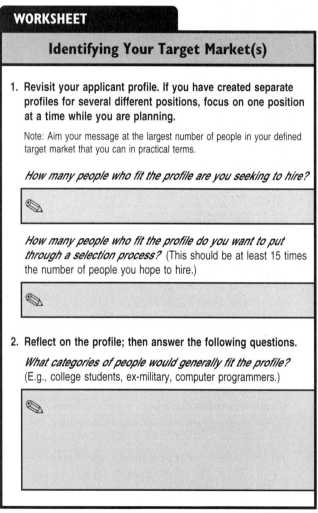

**WORKSHEET**

## Identifying Your Target Market(s)

1. Revisit your applicant profile. If you have created separate profiles for several different positions, focus on one position at a time while you are planning.

   Note: Aim your message at the largest number of people in your defined target market that you can in practical terms.

   *How many people who fit the profile are you seeking to hire?*

   *How many people who fit the profile do you want to put through a selection process?* (This should be at least 15 times the number of people you hope to hire.)

2. Reflect on the profile; then answer the following questions.

   *What categories of people would generally fit the profile?* (E.g., college students, ex-military, computer programmers.)

(Continued)

**WORKSHEET** (Concluded)

## Identifying Your Target Market(s)

*(More about who would generally fit the profile)*

*Who else would fit the profile?*

*Where are you likely to find large concentrations of people who fit the profile?* In a particular location or region? Airplanes or business hotels? College/University campuses? Working for your competition? In bookstores? In databases? Elsewhere?

## ➡ Identify the Best Means of Communicating With Your Target Market(s)

1. What is the best *direct* way to communicate with your audience?

2. What is the best *indirect* way to communicate with your audience?

Methods of direct communication include:

— Speaking with people at a planned event

— Telephoning, faxing, mailing, and e-mailing people

Methods of indirect communication include:

— Airing your message on radio and television

— Bringing your message to people in a Web publication, newspaper, or magazine

In what *specific ways* can you employ these methods to best communicate with your target market(s)? That is . . .

*Exactly what do you have in mind?*

---

*Use the following worksheet to start planning your campaign.*

---

**WORKSHEET**

## Identifying the Best Means of Communication

| METHODS | *Exactly What Do You Have in Mind?* |
|---|---|
| In Person: At a Planned Event | |
| In Person: At an Event You Host | |
| Telephone | |
| Fax | |
| Mail | |

(Continued)

**WORKSHEET** (Concluded)

## Identifying the Best Means of Communication

| METHODS | *Exactly What Do You Have in Mind?* |
|---|---|
| E-mail | |
| Radio | |
| Television | |
| Web Publication | |
| Newspaper | |
| Magazine | |

## ➡ Determine Your Resources

What resources can you mobilize for the campaign?
It is important to identify *all* of the resources that
are available to you.

*The following worksheet will help you
plan to mobilize resources for your campaign.*

---

**WORKSHEET**

### Determining Your Available Resources

■ PEOPLE. *Who can you get assigned to help you? Who will
volunteer?*

■ INFORMATION. *What lists can you get your hands on?*

(Continued)

## WORKSHEET (Concluded)

### Determining Your Available Resources

■ MONEY. *How many different budgets can you tap?*

■ SPACE. *What are all the possibilities for a campaign headquarters?*

■ MATERIALS. *How much can you requisition? How much can you scavenge?*

■ OTHER RESOURCES.

## ➡ Plan and Execute the Campaign

An effective campaign has four basic elements:

1.  **Unpaid media:** News or quasi-news coverage
2.  **Paid media:** Advertising
3.  **Direct contact:** Mail, telephone, fax, e-mail
4.  **Events:** Sponsored by you or someone else

Use the timetable on the next two pages to begin planning your goals for these campaign elements in the months ahead.

Subsequent worksheets in this section will help you zero in on the details of each element.

-   *Unpaid and paid media:* What media outlets will you consider?

-   *Unpaid media:* Compiling key information about unpaid-media outlets; the strategic approach to unpaid media

-   *Paid media:* Compiling key information about paid-media outlets; the strategic approach to paid media; organizing your advertising

-   *Direct contact:* Strategy; organizing direct contact

-   *Events:* Organizing events

## WORKSHEET

### Timetable: Overview of Basic Goals

| MONTH | UNPAID MEDIA | PAID MEDIA | DIRECT CONTACT | EVENTS |  |  |
|-------|--------------|------------|----------------|--------|--|--|
| JAN   |              |            |                |        |  |  |
| FEB   |              |            |                |        |  |  |
| MARCH |              |            |                |        |  |  |
| APRIL |              |            |                |        |  |  |
| MAY   |              |            |                |        |  |  |
| JUNE  |              |            |                |        |  |  |

(Continued)

## WORKSHEET (Concluded)

### Timetable: Overview of Basic Goals

| MONTH | UNPAID MEDIA | PAID MEDIA | DIRECT CONTACT | EVENTS | | | |
|---|---|---|---|---|---|---|---|
| JULY | | | | | | | |
| AUG | | | | | | | |
| SEPT | | | | | | | |
| OCT | | | | | | | |
| NOV | | | | | | | |
| DEC | | | | | | | |

## ☑ PAID AND UNPAID MEDIA

Your next step is to list all of the media outlets you will consider for paid and/or unpaid media.

### List of Media Outlets

| TELEVISION | RADIO | WEB |
|---|---|---|
|  |  |  |

| MAGAZINES | NEWSPAPERS |
|---|---|
|  |  |

## ☑ UNPAID MEDIA

You will need *key information* in dealing with unpaid-media outlets. You will also need *an effective strategy.*

### Unpaid-Media Outlets: Key Information

Build a database that includes these necessities:

- Contact information on journalists and editors—for example, their phone and fax numbers, mail and e-mail addresses

- Deadline information—for example, filing times for press media and broadcast times for broadcast media

- Details on the outlet's key editorial policies and procedures

- Special considerations—for example, whether or not the particular media outlet has call-in shows, talk shows, or special columns

---

*Use the following worksheet to record and organize your key information.*

---

**WORKSHEET**

## Unpaid-Media Outlets: Key Information

| MEDIA OUTLET | KEY CONTACT INFORMATION | DEADLINES | POLICIES AND PROCEDURES | SPECIAL CONSIDERATIONS |
|---|---|---|---|---|
|  |  |  |  |  |
|  |  |  |  |  |
|  |  |  |  |  |
|  |  |  |  |  |
|  |  |  |  |  |
|  |  |  |  |  |

**Unpaid Media: Strategy**

You will need to develop concrete news stories or events to pitch to editors and reporters. Build a list of the potentially reportable events connected to your recruiting program and all of the news angles that could be taken on the program. For instance:

- *"This year we are hiring 10 percent more people than last year."*

- *"This year we are having only our first-year employees conduct interviews."*

- *"This year we are giving out puppies to our interviewees."*

Designate as your recruiting spokesperson someone inside the company or an outsider who has name recognition and credibility with your target audience. If you are operating on the low-budget end, don't dismiss such tactics as letters to the editor and calls to phone-in talk shows.

The steps below sum up your best course of action.

*Generating a News Story: Key Steps*

➤ Find an angle or event that is newsworthy.

➤ Write a news release that is brief and focused on the points you consider most newsworthy.

➤ Consider assembling a news packet and sending it along with the news release. This packet would include photographs, documentation, and other supporting items.

➤ Send the news release early enough to give a news editor time to assign a reporter to cover the story. (Don't forget to include the news packet if you've assembled one.)

➤ Always follow up a news release with a telephone call to every person to whom you sent the release.

In addition, be sure to keep track of your results: Did your news release (and other any materials) generate a news story?

---

*The following worksheet will help you organize your strategic approach to generating news stories.*

---

## WORKSHEET

**Unpaid-Media Outlets: Generating News Stories**

| NEWS STORY Why newsworthy? | CONTENTS OF NEWS PACKET | EDITORS & REPORTERS TO GET PACKET & WHEN | FOLLOW-UP CALL & WHEN | RESULT Story? Yes/No |
|---|---|---|---|---|
| | | | | |
| | | | | |
| | | | | |
| | | | | |
| | | | | |
| | | | | |

# ☑ PAID MEDIA

You will also need *key information* in dealing with paid-media outlets. *An effective strategy,* including good organization, is also essential.

## Paid-Media Outlets: Key Information

Build a database that includes these necessities:

- Contact information for advertising representatives — particularly their phone and fax numbers, and mail and e-mail addresses.

- Price schedules

- Deadline information for purchasing ads — the number of days prior to running the ad

- Deadline information for delivering ad copy — again, the number of days prior to running the ad

---

*Use the following worksheet to record and organize your key information.*

---

## WORKSHEET

### Paid-Media Outlets: Key Information

| MEDIA OUTLET | KEY CONTACT INFORMATION | PRICE SCHEDULES | DEADLINE FOR PURCHASE | DEADLINE FOR AD-COPY DELIVERY |
|---|---|---|---|---|
| | | | | |
| | | | | |
| | | | | |
| | | | | |
| | | | | |
| | | | | |

## Paid Media: Strategy

When it comes to advertising, you may want to include an outside professional, but the bottom line is this: media outlets that sell advertising will provide you with a lot of support in the process because they want to make it easy for you to spend money advertising in their sphere. Remember, the key to an effective ad in any media is being disciplined about sticking to the message — if you've done the market research and developed a powerful message, just repeat that message again and again.

Here are some other tips for creating ads:

- **Print ads.** When designing an ad, use a big picture (photo or graphic) and as few words as possible (just the message and contact information). The publication's ad department will follow whatever copy and layout you specify.

- **Radio.** Write a script for a sixty-second spot (read it slowly, timing yourself) and then go to the radio station. Usually, the people there will put you in a recording studio to read the ad yourself or, if you prefer, have a voice-over person read it. They will also put music behind the ad and may have some fun suggestions.

- **Television.** Producing a spot can get quite complicated, but these days, especially with cable television, it's a whole lot easier than it used to be. Your local cable vendor probably has an internal advertising department or internal agency that can work with you to shoot footage, edit a thirty-second spot, and help you buy television time.

  Advertising in local markets on CNN, A&E, ESPN, and other networks allows you to get your message on television inexpensively and penetrate very localized markets.

- **Web.** Most sites that take ads will advise you on the process, but keep in mind the advice offered above for print ads. The fewer words you use, the better. The best result with a Web ad is to get a link to your own website.

---

*Organization is an important part of this strategy.*

*The following tools will help you keep track of your paid-media advertising plans and the basics for print, radio, television, and Web ads.*

---

## ORGANIZER

### Paid-Media Advertising Organizer

| MEDIA | Number of Outlets | Budget | Time Frame |
|---|---|---|---|
| *Print* | | | |
| *Radio* | | | |
| *Television* | | | |
| *Web* | | | |

## ORGANIZER

### Print Advertising Buying Organizer

| PUBLICATION | TARGET DATES | AD SIZE | COST PER AD | NO. OF ADS | COST PER PUBLICATION | RUNNING TOTAL |
|---|---|---|---|---|---|---|
| | | | | | | |
| | | | | | | |
| | | | | | | |
| | | | | | | |
| | | | | | | |
| | | | | | | |

## ORGANIZER

### Radio Advertising Buying Organizer

| STATION | START DATE | END DATE | COST PER AD | TOTAL NO. ADS | PER DAY NO. ADS | COST PER STATION | RUNNING TOTAL |
|---------|-----------|----------|-------------|---------------|-----------------|------------------|---------------|
|         |           |          |             |               |                 |                  |               |
|         |           |          |             |               |                 |                  |               |
|         |           |          |             |               |                 |                  |               |
|         |           |          |             |               |                 |                  |               |
|         |           |          |             |               |                 |                  |               |
|         |           |          |             |               |                 |                  |               |

## ORGANIZER

### Television Advertising Buying Organizer

| NETWORK | START DATE | END DATE | COST PER AD | TOTAL NO. ADS | PER DAY NO. ADS | COST PER NETWORK | RUNNING TOTAL |
|---------|-----------|----------|-------------|---------------|-----------------|------------------|---------------|
|         |           |          |             |               |                 |                  |               |
|         |           |          |             |               |                 |                  |               |
|         |           |          |             |               |                 |                  |               |
|         |           |          |             |               |                 |                  |               |
|         |           |          |             |               |                 |                  |               |
|         |           |          |             |               |                 |                  |               |

## ORGANIZER

### Web Advertising Buying Organizer

| WEBSITE | START DATE | END DATE | TOTAL NO. ADS | AD CONTENT & FORMAT | COST PER AD | COST PER SITE | RUNNING TOTAL |
|---------|-----------|----------|---------------|---------------------|-------------|---------------|---------------|
|  |  |  |  |  |  |  |  |
|  |  |  |  |  |  |  |  |
|  |  |  |  |  |  |  |  |
|  |  |  |  |  |  |  |  |
|  |  |  |  |  |  |  |  |
|  |  |  |  |  |  |  |  |

# ☑ DIRECT CONTACT

There are five possible ways to make direct contact with your target applicants: by telephone, fax, mail, and e-mail, and in person. The key to any effective strategy is being in control of a database with the correct contact information.

The process of direct contact has three main steps:

1. Identify and secure available databases with contact information.

2. Decide on how many people you'll need to contact to attract the number of applicants you want. (Try to contact at least 100 times the number of applicants you are seeking.)

3. Decide on what type of direct contact will be most effective for reaching those people.

---

*Use the tool on the next two pages to organize your contacts by month and type of contact.*

---

Here are some useful tips for direct contact:

- **Telephone.** Build a team or hire a phone bank that will phone potential applicants and let them know about the career opportunity you have to offer.

## ORGANIZER

### Direct-Contact Organizer

| MONTH | NO. PEOPLE CONTACTED (From what database?) | PHONE | FAX | MAIL | E-MAIL | EVENTS |
|-------|-------------------------------------------|-------|-----|------|--------|--------|
| JAN | | | | | | |
| FEB | | | | | | |
| MARCH | | | | | | |
| APRIL | | | | | | |
| MAY | | | | | | |
| JUNE | | | | | | |

(Continued)

## ORGANIZER (Concluded)

### Direct-Contact Organizer

| MONTH | NO. PEOPLE CONTACTED (From what database?) | PHONE | FAX | MAIL | E-MAIL | EVENTS |
|---|---|---|---|---|---|---|
| JULY | | | | | | |
| AUG | | | | | | |
| SEPT | | | | | | |
| OCT | | | | | | |
| NOV | | | | | | |
| DEC | | | | | | |

- **Fax.** This is a low-cost way to get printed information to people, but some people are hard to reach by fax and many faxes are not secure.

- **Mail.** You can send personal letters, glossy brochures, or simple postcards. Handle the mailing yourself, or contract a direct-mail firm.

- **E-mail.** This form of communication is very personal, so can be very effective; but be careful about imposing. One approach is to invite people to visit a special recruiting website.

- **Personal meetings.** The best way to meet with people in person is to participate in or host an event that draws a crowd of potential applicants (see "Events" section below).

## ☑ EVENTS

When it comes to planning events, ask yourself: *What can I do to make the event special?* For example, in one case, an employer (a large toy-store chain) set up a huge inflatable playground at an on-campus recruiting event. And don't forget the potential news/publicity tie-in!

---

*The following organizational tool will help you with your event planning.*

---

## ORGANIZER

### Event Planning Organizer

✓ *What is going to make this event special?*

✓ *What is going to make this event newsworthy?*

| PARTICULARS | PERSON RESPONSIBLE | DEADLINE |
|---|---|---|
| Location | | |
| Date | | |
| Refreshments | | |
| Programming | | |
| Invitation List | | |
| Invitations (produced & sent) | | |
| Follow-up Calls | | |

## ➡ Managing the Campaign

The effective management of a campaign includes these three essentials:

- Managing the campaign team
- Planning a budget
- Updating your campaign timetable

## ☑ MANAGING THE TEAM

Manage the campaign team as you would any other results-oriented team:

- Assign every tangible result to an owner.

- Ensure that every result-owner accepts 100 percent responsibility at the time of delegation.

- Attach a concrete deadline to every tangible result, regardless of scope.

- Spell out all the parameters, guidelines, and specifications at the time that results and deadlines are assigned.

- Hold people responsible for the results.

---

*The following organizational tool will help you manage your campaign team effectively.*

---

**ORGANIZER**

## Managing the Campaign Team

| RESULT | OWNER | DEADLINE | GUIDELINES & PARAMETERS |
|--------|-------|----------|-------------------------|
|        |       |          |                         |
|        |       |          |                         |
|        |       |          |                         |
|        |       |          |                         |
|        |       |          |                         |
|        |       |          |                         |
|        |       |          |                         |
|        |       |          |                         |

## ☑ PLANNING A BUDGET AND UPDATING YOUR TIMETABLE

Finally, you will need to plan a recruiting budget and update your timetable for executing the delivery of the campaign message. The two organizing tools that conclude this chapter have been designed to help you get through these last planning steps easily and effectively.

The **budget planner** on the next page lists expense items and gives you room to record the total amount of each item and the date when the expenditures will be made.

The **campaign timetable** that follows it allows you to plan the events of the campaign month by month. This organizing tool matches the worksheet you used at the beginning of the campaign-planning process to create an overview of your goals for the campaign. At this point in the planning process, you should be able to create a more detailed overview and get a better picture of the campaign.

---

*Once you reach this point in planning, you should be ready to set the campaign into motion!*

---

**ORGANIZER**

## Planning Your Budget

| EXPENSE ITEMS | TOTAL | WHEN EXPENDITURE WILL BE MADE |
|---|---|---|
| Administrative expense: personnel, equipment, utilities, supplies | | |
| Database acquisition, tailoring, maintenance | | |
| Survey research: focus groups, polling, etc. | | |
| Mailing materials and supplies | | |
| Telephone, fax, e-mail costs | | |
| Paid advertising | | |
| Unpaid media | | |
| Events | | |

## ORGANIZER

### Timetable: Overview of the Campaign

| MONTH | UNPAID MEDIA | PAID MEDIA | DIRECT CONTACT | EVENTS |
|-------|--------------|------------|----------------|--------|
| JAN | | | | |
| FEB | | | | |
| MARCH | | | | |
| APRIL | | | | |
| MAY | | | | |
| JUNE | | | | |

(Continued)

## ORGANIZER (Concluded)

### Timetable: Overview of the Campaign

| MONTH | UNPAID MEDIA | PAID MEDIA | DIRECT CONTACT | EVENTS | | | |
|-------|-------------|-----------|----------------|--------|--|--|--|
| JULY  |             |           |                |        |  |  |  |
| AUG   |             |           |                |        |  |  |  |
| SEPT  |             |           |                |        |  |  |  |
| OCT   |             |           |                |        |  |  |  |
| NOV   |             |           |                |        |  |  |  |
| DEC   |             |           |                |        |  |  |  |

# Selecting for Skill and Performance

THE BIGGEST PROBLEM WITH SELECTION PRACTICES in today's tight labor market is that employers are so desperate to hire people, the only selection criterion is "Do you have a pulse?" The goal of developing a compelling recruiting message and running an effective recruiting campaign is to attract an applicant pool large enough to let you be selective. Don't sell applicants all the way *in* the door; rather, sell them all the way *up to* the door. Then you can "select out" the candidates who don't fit your needs and "select in" the ones who do.

In the workplace of the past, the key to selection was identifying good prospects for long-term employment: Will this person join the corporate family, hitch his or her wagon to your star, pay the required dues, and climb the ladder? Applicants were expected to send in a cover letter with a resume and wait to hear from you. If the resume demonstrated a sufficient background of education and experience, you would call to schedule the applicant for an initial interview. If the applicant passed muster, you would call him or her back for an extensive set of interviews with some key decision-makers. Perhaps you would ask for a letter of reference from a previous employer.

In the workplace of today — which is also the workplace of the future — you are not looking for people to join the family and climb the corporate ladder. Now you need people who bring specific skills to the table and can get up to speed quickly and start making valuable contributions right away. Cover letters and resumes don't tell you much about a person. Interviews aren't as reliable as they used to be because so many people are practicing how to give the "right" answers in job interviews — the kind of answers "interviewers want to hear." And you can't trust letters of reference because everybody is afraid of getting sued.

## ⊶ THE KEY

Develop a selection process that focuses on skill and performance criteria. Collect as much proof as you can that potential hires have the skills they need to get up to speed quickly and start contributing right away.

## ➤ THE PROCESS

- Before engaging in the selection process, revisit the skill-and-performance-based profile for the position you want to fill.

- Ask your applicants to submit detailed proposals outlining exactly how they intend to add value in your organization.

- Focus interviews on skill and performance criteria; when possible, first get a sample of each applicant's work product.

- Design a job preview to give applicants a realistic picture of what the experience of the job will be like.

### ➤ Revisit the Job Profile's Key Elements

1. What are the tasks and responsibilities?

2. What skills are needed?

3. What credentials are essential?

*Use the following worksheet to revisit the profile.*

## WORKSHEET

### Revisiting Key Elements of Job Profile

| Tasks & Responsibilities | Required Skills | Required Credentials |
|---|---|---|
|  |  |  |

## ➤ Ask Applicants for Proposals

Word your proposal request in this way: *"Please submit a detailed proposal outlining exactly how you intend to add value in our organization."* You may want to say no more and see what applicants come up with on their own. This will tell you a lot about the resourcefulness of your applicants and give you an idea of how they see your needs, their skills, and the potential marriage of your needs and their skills.

Of course, you may prefer to give applicants some guidance in creating their proposals. Guidelines for this alternative approach include:

- Explaining your organization's needs

- Asking applicant to describe how his or her skills address those needs and how applicant intends to apply the skills

- Having applicant propose a timetable of goals and deadlines for accomplishing those goals

- Asking what resources would be needed to meet goals, what obstacles might interfere, and how applicant would overcome the obstacles

*The following is a helpful form for this process.*

# Applicant Proposal Guidelines

*Our organization has the following needs:*

_____

_____

_____

_____

1. Please describe your skills as they address the needs above.

_____

_____

_____

_____

2. How do you intend to apply your skills to address the needs above? Exactly what do you intend to do? How? Why?

_____

_____

_____

_____

**3.** Please propose a timetable of goals and deadlines.

| GOALS | DEADLINES |
|-------|-----------|
|       |           |
|       |           |
|       |           |
|       |           |
|       |           |

**4.** What resources do you anticipate needing to accomplish these goals?

_____

_____

_____

**5.** What obstacles do you anticipate encountering and how would you overcome them?

_____

_____

_____

## ➡ Focus Interviews on Skill and Performance Criteria

Too many employers conduct interviews that are unfocused or, even worse, focused on irrelevant or inappropriate subject matter. I've heard stories about interviewers asking applicants inappropriate questions such as "What was it like growing up in your family?" and "Do you intend to have children?" I've also heard stories about interviewers asking stupid questions like "What can you do in the next sixty seconds that will really impress me?"

A surprising number of interviewers simply go through an applicant's resume on the spot, reading it aloud (often, reading it for the first time), asking for amplification here and clarification there. Many just want to "get to know the applicant" by chatting informally about sports or clothes or classes the applicant took in college. Other interviewers explicitly waste the interview by doing all of the talking themselves instead of hearing from (and listening to) the applicants.

## ☑ INTERVIEW GUIDELINES

The best indication of the kind of work people are going to do for you is some evidence of the kind of work they have done for others (or themselves).

In advance of interviews, ask applicants to provide you with "samples" of tangible results they have produced, and make sure you can verify that the work was done by the applicants.

Whether or not an applicant has provided a work sample, focus interview questions on specific instances of work experience. As the interviewee talks about these specific instances, guide the discussion to specific skill and performance criteria.

Below is a simple format for interviewing based on skill and performance.

## ☑ INTERVIEW FORMAT

### Performance

1. Please tell me about a specific instance when you did [INSERT PERFORMANCE].

   EXAMPLES:

   - Identified a specific type of problem
   - Solved a specific type of problem
   - Accomplished a particular task
   - Were charged with a particular kind of responsibility
   - Worked in a particular type of situation
   - Worked in a particular set of conditions

2. What was successful about your approach?

3. What was unsuccessful about your approach?

4. What did you learn?

5. What would you do differently?

6. Let me describe to you a specific instance when, if you worked for us, you would have to do [INSERT PERFORMANCE SIMILAR TO THAT SPECIFIED IN ITEM 1].

   *How would you approach the challenge?*

## Skill

1. Please tell me about a specific instance when you utilized [INSERT SKILL].

2. What was successful about your approach?

3. What was unsuccessful about your approach?

4. What did you learn?

5. What would you do differently?

6. What ancillary skills were useful?

7. How have you developed this skill further since then?

8. In the specific instance you described, what related skill did you utilize?

9. What was successful about your approach?

10. What was unsuccessful about your approach?

11. What did you learn?

12. What would you do differently?

13. How have you developed this related skill further since then?

14. Let me describe to you a specific instance when, if you worked for us, you would have to utilize [INSERT THE SKILL SPECIFIED IN ITEM 1].

    *How would you approach the challenge?*

15. Let me describe to you a specific instance when, if you worked for us, you would have to utilize [INSERT THE SKILL SPECIFIED IN ITEM 7].

    *How would you approach the challenge?*

## ➡ Design a Realistic Preview of the Job

One of the most common causes of voluntary turn-over is unmet expectations—new employees finding out that the job they were hired to do is not exactly what they had envisioned when they applied.

This problem can be remedied if, once you select the applicants who seem most suitable for the position, you provide an accurate preview of the day-to-day experience of accomplishing the tasks and meeting the responsibilities required by the position — negatives as well as positives. Plus, job previews allow you to get a final look at applicants in the context of the actual work you will be hiring one of them to do.

# ☑ JOB-PREVIEW GUIDELINES

## Methods

There are many ways to provide accurate job previews, including the following:

1. Offer the applicant you wish to select the opportunity to "tag along" with an employee who is doing the same job (or a similar one). By tagging along for several days, a week, or more, your applicant will get a good picture of what the job actually entails.

2. Offer internships to potential applicants.

3. Produce a videotape, audiotape, or CD-ROM of people in your organization performing the key tasks and responsibilities of the job; then give your applicants an opportunity to review it.

4. Create a print document to achieve results similar to the above, but at a lower cost; then give applicants a chance to review it.

5. Encourage applicants to engage in frank discussions with you or your employees about the low points as well as the high points of the position you are seeking to fill.

### Preparation

When preparing the job preview, always be sure to consider these questions:

- What information should be included in a realistic preview of the job for which you are considering the applicant?

   — *What are the negatives?*
   — *What are the positives?*

- What else would be difficult to know about the job until one actually did it?

- What is the best format for the preview, considering the answers to the questions above?

---

*The following worksheet is a useful tool for preparing an effective preview of the job.*

---

## WORKSHEET

### Preparing the Job Preview

CONTENT: *What information should be communicated in the preview?*

| NEGATIVES | POSITIVES | WHAT ELSE? |
|-----------|-----------|------------|
|           |           |            |

FORMAT: *Given that this information must be communicated, what is the best format for the preview?*

# A Quick
# Recruiting Review

**WITH EMPLOYERS IN EVERY INDUSTRY** spending so much
time, energy, and money trying to bring in the talent
they need, there is tremendous pressure on everyone who is involved in recruiting. The competition
for talent today is almost as intense as the competition for customers.

The fundamental message of *Recruiting the Workforce of the Future* is that employers should no
longer be recruiting for the long term, but rather,
recruiting to get the job done *today, tomorrow, and
next week*. This pocket guide has conveyed that
message by focusing on best practices in four areas:

> ➤ 1. **Profiling**
> ➤ 2. **The Recruiting Message**
> ➤ 3. **The Recruiting Campaign**
> ➤ 4. **Selection**

In this chapter, we'll review the best practices in
each area.

# I. PROFILING

 In the workplace of the future, it is critical to discard obsolete recruiting and hiring criteria. The only thing that matters is this: Can the person get the work done—accomplish the results you need—quickly and at a high level of quality? Profiling should be based *only* on skill and performance criteria.

- Reassess traditional credential requirements for each task and responsibility.

  (You may find that many of the necessary tasks and responsibilities do not, in fact, require any particular credentials.)

- Develop profiles on the basis of skill and performance criteria.

- Brainstorm using the checklist of critical skills for workers of the future, provided in Chapter 1.

Remember, there are three sets of critical skills:

1. **Learning skills.** *These include such skills as multi-tasking and critical thinking.*

2. **Relationship skills.** *For example, empathy, trustworthiness, communication, and being a mentor.*

3. **Value-adding skills.** *Among them, problem solving, strategic planning, going the extra mile, flexibility, and adaptability.*

## 2. THE RECRUITING MESSAGE

Create a compelling recruiting message by answering the number one question of potential recruits:

### What's the deal?

*Or: Exactly what do you want me to do today, tomorrow, next week, and this month; and exactly what do you have to offer me in the form of financial and nonfinancial rewards today, tomorrow, next week, and this month?*

- Evaluate your traditional rewards; then identify the ones that vest in the near term.

- Brainstorm the incentives you have to offer.

Using the eight factors that matter most to workers of the future, brainstorm incentives, particularly those you have to offer in the near term.

- Clarify exactly what you want from the person you are hiring.

- Develop a "What's the Deal?" recruiting message for each position that you are selling.

Remember, these are the eight factors that matter most to workers of the future:

1. *Performance-Based Compensation*

2. *Flexible Schedules*

3. *Flexible Location*

4. *Training and Learning Opportunities— Marketable Skills*

5. *Access to Decision-Makers*

6. *Credit for Results Achieved*

7. *Clear Area of Responsibility*

8. *Creative Freedom*

# 3. THE RECRUITING CAMPAIGN

The goal of any recruiting campaign is quite simple:

*Deliver the most compelling message to large concentrations of potential employees in order to draw them into your applicant pool.*

- Identify your target market(s). Decide who will be the audience for your message: Can you describe the market(s) in specific terms?

- Identify the best means of direct and indirect communication with your target market(s).

- Determine your resources: What resources will be available to run the campaign?

- Plan and execute the campaign.

- Manage the campaign.

An effective campaign has four main elements:

1. *Unpaid Media*
2. *Paid Media*
3. *Direct Contact*
4. *Events*

# 4. SELECTION

 Develop a selection process that focuses on skill and performance criteria. Collect as much proof as you can that potential hires have the skills they need to get up to speed quickly and start contributing right away.

- Before engaging in the selection process, revisit the skill-and-performance-based profile for the position you are seeking to fill.

- Ask applicants to submit detailed proposals outlining exactly how the applicant intends to add value in your organization.

- Focus interviews on skill and performance criteria; whenever possible, first get a sample of each applicant's work product.

- Design a job preview to give applicants a realistic picture of exactly what the experience of the job will be like.

## In Conclusion

I hope you found this second edition of *Recruiting the Workforce of the Future* to be clear and simple, practical and "actionable." It is my greatest hope that you will be able to apply these best practices and tools for recruiting and bring in the talent you need to get the work done in your organization.

# — APPENDIX

# Web-Based Recruiting Resources

## Introduction

The key advantage to Web-based recruiting services is that they revolve around proprietary databases of job seekers and/or job postings. Those that focus on job-seeker databases enable employers to search databases with specified criteria, often including skill, experience, location, academic background, and other factors.

The benefit for employers is that, for a fee, these searches yield substantial lists of potential applicants, all of whom have gone to the trouble to list their information with a service. Contacting the applicants and selecting from among them is still the employer's burden, although some of the more sophisticated services offer resources to help with this process. Most of the services that allow employers to list job postings are easy to work with, and your postings are set up just like classified ads.

The following list is not only a great starting place for investigating what Web-based recruiting services can do for you, but also a useful reference tool that you can return to again and again. The services have been put into alphabetical order using the letter-by-letter system, with numerical names listed according to their letter equivalent.

## Please note!

Due to the transitory nature of many sites on the Web, the listed URLs are subject to change.

# List of Major Recruiting Websites

Adguide's College Recruiter
Employment Site ............... www.collegerecruiter.com

Alumni-Network .................. www.alumni-network.com

American Home Labor
Force .................................... www.netfit.com/employment/

American Jobs .................... www.americanjobs.com

American Preferred Jobs .... www.preferredjobs.com

America's Job Bank ............ www.jobsearch.org

ArtHire ................................. www.arthire.com

Asian American
Economic Development
Enterprises, Inc. .................. www.aaede.org

Atlanta Job Resource
Center ................................. www.ajrc.com

Best Jobs USA .................... www.bestjobsusa.com

BrassRing ........................... www.brassring.com

Canada Centre .................. www.canadacentre.com/jobscan/

Canada-Wide ...................... www.canada-wide.com

Capital Region
ReEmployment Center ....... www.crrc.com

## Major Recruiting Websites cont.

| | |
|---|---|
| Career and Resume Management for the 21st Century | www.crm21.com |
| Career Avenue | www.careeravenue.com |
| CareerBuilder | www.careerbuilder.com |
| CareerCast | www.careercast.com |
| CareerCity | www.careercity.com |
| Career.com | www.career.com |
| Career Connector | www.careerconnector.com |
| CareerExchange | www.careerexchange.com |
| Career Exposure | www.careerexposure.com |
| CareerFairs | www.careerfairs.com |
| CareerGuide | www.careerguide.com |
| CareerHighway | www.careerhighway.com |
| Careerjournal | www.careerjournal.com |
| CareerMagazine | www.careermag.com |
| CareerMarketplace Network | www.careermarketplace.com |
| CareerMart | www.careermart.com |
| CareerMatrix | www.careermatrix.com |
| CareerMosaic | www.careermosaic.com |
| Career Moves | www.jvsjobs.org |
| Careernet | www.careernet.com |
| CareerPark | www.careerpark.com |
| CareerPath.com | www.careerpath.com |

Career Resource Center .... www.careers.org

CareerShop ........................ www.careershop.com

CareerSite .......................... www.careersite.com

Careers OnLine ................. www.careersonline.com

CareerSource Magazine ..... www.careersource-
magazine.com

Careers2000.net ................ www.careers2000.net

Centre for Advancement
in Work and Living, The ...... www.cawl.org

CHOICE ............................. www.choicecareer.com

Christian Jobs Online ......... www.christianjobs.com

Cidron PeopleBank ............. www.cidronpeoplebank.com

Classified Employment
Website .............................. www.yourinfosource.com/
clews/

College Central Network .... www.collegecentral.com

College Grad Job Hunter .... www.collegegrad.com

Contract Employment
Weekly ............................... www.ceweekly.wa.com

Cool Jobs ........................... www.cooljobs.com

Creative Central ................. www.creativecentral.com

Cruel World ........................ www.cruelworld.com

Cyberia Jobs Database ...... www.cyberiacafe.net

Design Automation Café ..... www.dacafe.com

Dice.com ............................ www.dice.com

Direct-Jobs ........................ www.direct-jobs.com

E-job ................................... www.e-job.net

## Major Recruiting Websites cont.

Ejob ..................................... www.ejob.com

ELECTRICjob.com ............. www.electricjob.com

Employment Guide's
CareerWeb, The ................. www.cweb.com

Erp-jobs.com ....................... www.erp-jobs.com

ExeCon Information
System ............................... www.execonweb.com

Exec-U-Net ......................... www.execunet.com

1st Resume Store
International ........................ www.resumestore.com

Fortuna ............................... .fortuna.frinet.org

4work .................................. www.4work.com

FreetimeJobs ...................... www.freetimejobs.com

Future Access Employment
Guide .................................. www.futureaccess.com

GO Jobs .............................. www.gojobs.com

GroupWeb Employment
Services .............................. www.groupweb.com/opening/
jobs.htm

Headhunter.net ................... www.headhunter.net

Helpwanted.com ................. www.helpwanted.com

Help-Wanted Page, The ..... www.helpwantedpage.com

Hire.com .............................. www.hire.com

HotJobs ............................... www.hotjobs.com

HVACjob.com ...................... www.hvacjob.com

IDEAS Job Network ............ www.ideasjn.com

Internet Business
Network ............................... www.interbiznet.com

Internet Career Connection  www.iccweb.com

Internet Job Locator, The ... www.joblocator.com

IWantWork.com .................. www.iwantwork.com

JobBank USA ..................... www.jobbankusa.com

JobDirect ............................ www.jobdirect.com

Jobfind ............................... www.jobfind.com

JobForce Network, The ...... www.jobforce.net

JobFront ............................. www.jobfront.com

Job Getter .......................... www.rvp.com/jh/

Job-Hunt.Org ..................... www.job-hunt.org

Job Link USA ..................... www.joblink-usa.com

JobOptions ......................... www.joboptions.com

JOBPLACE ........................ www.jobplace.com

Job Resource, The ............. www.thejobresource.com

JobSafari ............................ www.jobsafari.com

Jobs & Adverts
Jobpilot .............................. usa.jobpilot.com

Jobs & Careers
Newspaper ......................... www.jobscareers.com

Jobs-Careers ..................... www.jobs-careers.com

JobsJobsJobs ..................... www.jobsjobsjobs.com

JobsOnTheWeb .................. www.jobsontheweb.com

JobWarehouse .................... www.jobwarehouse.com

Jobz ................................... www.jobz.ozware.com

## Major Recruiting Websites cont.

LatPro ............................... www.latpro.com

MBAFreeAgents ................ www.mbafreeagents.com

MinistrySearch ................... www.ministrysearch.com

Minorities' Job Bank .......... www.iminorities.com

Monster.com ...................... www.monster.com

NationJob Network ............ www.nationjob.com

Netpilgrim ........................... www.netpilgrim.com

Net-Temps ......................... www.net-temps.com

Online Help Wanted ........... www.ohw.com

Online-Jobs ........................ www.online-jobs.com

OnlineSports.com Career
Center ............................... www.onlinesports.com/pages/
                                                    careercenter.html

PeopleBank ....................... www.peoplebank.com

PLUMBjob.com ................... www.plumbjob.com

Price Jamieson .................. www.pricejam.com

Real Cities JobHunter ......... www.jobhunter.com

Recruitex ........................... www.recruitex.com

Resume Malaysia .............. www.resumemalaysia.com

Resumes On-Line .............. www.adpage.com/resumes/

Resunet ............................. www.resunet.com

Sales-Recruiter.com .......... www.sales-recruiter.com

Search Bulletin, The .......... www.searchbulletin.com

SearchEase ....................... www.searchease.com

Senior Staff, The ................ www.srstaff.com

Shop4Jobs ......................... www.shop4jobs.com

SocialService.Com ............. www.socialservice.com

Sunday Paper, The ............. www.sundaypaper.com

Tech-Engine ....................... www.tech-engine.com

Top Jobs on the Net ........... www.topjobs.net

Twin Cities Employment
Weekly .............................. www.getwork.com

Union Jobs
Clearinghouse .................... www.unionjobs.com

USApply ............................. www.usapply.com

US Careers Resource
Center ............................... www.uscareers.com

USJobLink ......................... www.usjoblink.com

Vault Job Board ................. www.vault.com

Visajobs ............................ www.visajobs.com

WorkAccess ....................... www.workaccess.com

WorkSeek Network ............. www.workseek.com

TheWorkSite.Com ............. www.theworksite.com

Works USA, The ................ www.theworksusa.com

Work-Web .......................... www.work-web.com

Yahoo! Classifieds ............. www.classifieds.yahoo.com